Do You Really Want To Create a Mudslide?

A Book About Erosion

ADVENTURES IN
SCIENCE

WRITTEN BY DANIEL D. MAURER · ILLUSTRATED BY TERESA ALBERINI

AMICUS ILLUSTRATED
is published by Amicus
P.O. Box 1329, Mankato, MN 56002
www.amicuspublishing.us

Paperback edition printed by RiverStream Publishing in arrangement with Amicus.
ISBN 978-1-62243-358-2 (paperback)

Library of Congress Cataloging-in-Publication Data
Names: Maurer, Daniel D., 1971- author. | Alberini, Teresa, illustrator.
Title: Do you really want to create a mudslide? : a book about erosion /
written by Daniel D. Maurer ; illustrated by Teresa Alberini.
Description: Mankato, Minnesota : Amicus, [2017] | Series: Amicus illustrated | Series:
Adventures in science | Audience: K to grade 3. |
Includes bibliographical references and index.
Identifiers: LCCN 2015040670 (print) | LCCN 2015041048 (ebook) | ISBN
9781607539575 (library binding : alk. paper) | ISBN 9781681510699 (eBook)
Subjects: LCSH: Erosion—Juvenile literature. | Mudslides—Juvenile
literature. | Weathering—Juvenile literature.
Classification: LCC QE599 M38 2017 (print) | LCC QE599 (ebook) | DDC 551.3/52—dc23
LC record available at http://lccn.loc.gov/2015040670

Editor: Rebecca Glaser
Designer: Kathleen Petelinsek

Printed in the United States of America at
Corporate Graphics in North Mankato, Minnesota.

HC 10 9 8 7 6 5 4 3 2 1
PB 10 9 8 7 6 5

ABOUT THE AUTHOR

Daniel D. Maurer writes for both children and adults and lives in Saint Paul, Minnesota with his wife, two boys, two cats, and one dog. They all dig science together. Visit *www.danthestoryman.com* to learn more.

ABOUT THE ILLUSTRATOR

Teresa Alberini has always loved painting and drawing. She attended the Academy of Fine Arts in Florence, Italy, and she now lives and works as an illustrator in a small town on the Italian coast. Visit her on the web at *www.teresaalberini.com.*

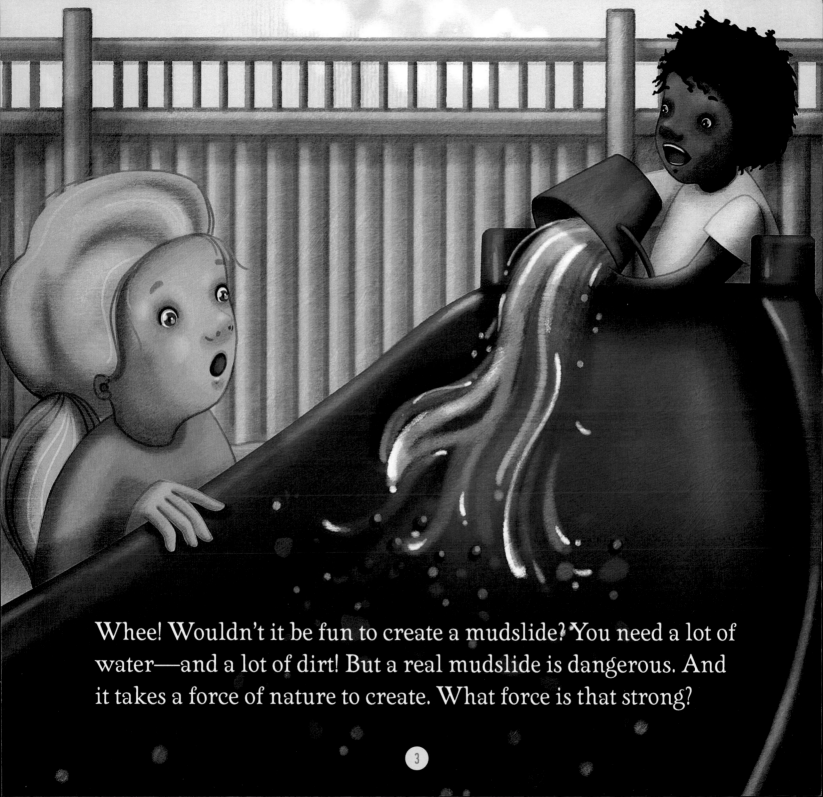

Whee! Wouldn't it be fun to create a mudslide? You need a lot of water—and a lot of dirt! But a real mudslide is dangerous. And it takes a force of nature to create. What force is that strong?

Erosion! Erosion is the natural process of moving soil and rock from one place to another. It changes the shape of the land.

Get ready for rain! In a mudslide, when the ground is soggy and heavy rains soak a steep hill, down goes the mud!

A mudslide is one of the fastest types of erosion. Mudslides are dangerous. The falling earth can block highways and train tracks. Some mudslides have even buried villages. You were lucky!

Other times, erosion happens much more slowly. For rock and soil to erode, there needs to be weathering. This process breaks down rock and soil into tiny pieces.

What shapes the land in this desert? The wind! It blows sand around and wears off tiny bits of soft rock. But this process takes a long time—millions of years.

Water can erode rock slowly, too. In a river, the water breaks off little bits of rock as it flows. It carries this sediment down the river. Flowing water can also erode the banks of the river.

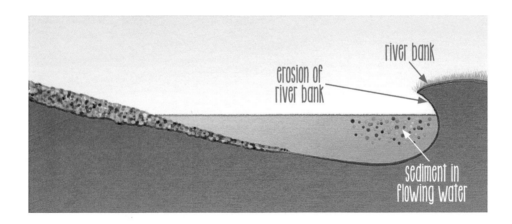

river bank

erosion of river bank

sediment in flowing water

The power of erosion is easy to see. The Grand Canyon in the U.S. state of Arizona was formed by erosion. Little by little, the river carried bits of rock away, and the canyon got deeper and deeper. It took millions of years!

What else can cause erosion?
Ice! In Alaska, you can see huge
sheets of ice called glaciers.
They move a few inches or
centimeters each year. As the
glaciers slide slowly down the
mountains, they take rocks and
soil with them.

Erosion is part of nature, but people change the land, too.
Plant and tree roots help hold the soil together.

When land is cleared for farming or logging, the soil is bare.
Then wind blows it away easily. Rain can wash it away, too.

Construction changes the land, too. When plants are cleared to build roads, topsoil can easily wash away. Replanting next to the road after it is done can help keep the soil in place.

Now that you know about erosion, you can try making a *little* mudslide—in your sandbox. You can leave the big ones to nature!

As rainwater flows, it gathers speed and mixes with soil and rocks to erode them. Create a mini-rainstorm with this experiment and see how soil erodes.

MINI-RAINSTORM EROSION

TRY THIS!

WHAT YOU NEED:

- Two 9x12 inch (23x30 cm) disposable aluminum casserole pans
- Dirt (soil from the ground, not potting soil)
- Three thick books
- Sharp-pointed scissors
- Watering can with sprinkler-style spout

WHAT YOU DO:

1. Have an adult poke eight small holes on the end of one pan with the scissors.
2. Fill the pan with dirt so it is about 2 inches (5 cm) deep. Smooth dirt evenly on the surface.
3. Prop up the pan with the dirt with two of the books. On the side with the holes, place the other aluminum pan below to catch the water and dirt.
4. Fill the watering can with water. Pour the water quickly and slowly. What happens to the dirt? If you wanted to prevent the soil from eroding, what could you do to slow or stop it?
5. Try adding one book to make a steeper slope. Does the dirt erode more or less? What does the water flowing through the holes look like?

Water is only one weathering agent—the wind is another. This experiment shows how the wind erodes different types of soil.

WHAT YOU NEED:

- Newspaper
- Two plastic disposable cups
- Play sand (from a sandbox)
- Garden soil
- Party balloon

WHAT YOU DO:

1. Cover your work surface with newspaper.
2. Fill one cup with play sand and the other with garden soil.
3. Add just enough water to the cup with sand to make it stand on its own.
   Press down the sand like you're making a sand castle. Turn the cup quickly on its end and remove the cup slowly so the structure stands on its own.
4. Add just a little water to the cup with dirt. It will take less water than the sand. (You don't want to make a mud pile!) Press down the dirt; then turn over the cup to make a dirt castle.
5. Allow your "castles" to dry for one hour.
6. For the wind, blow up a party balloon, but don't tie it. Point the balloon at each castle and let the air out. Which type of soil stands up better to the wind?
7. Try letting out the air at different distances. How does this affect the erosion of either castle?

23

GLOSSARY

canyon—A deep, narrow river valley with steep sides.

erosion—The natural process of moving soil and rock from one place to another; it changes the shape of the land.

glacier—A huge sheet of ice moving slowly down a mountain or valley.

mudslide—A fast-moving landslide in which a large mass of mud flows down a hill.

sediment—Small bits of matter such as dirt or rocks that can be carried by water to another place.

topsoil—The top layer of soil that has the most nutrients for growing plants.

weathering—The breaking down of soil, minerals, and rocks into small pieces as they come into contact with air, water, or ice.

READ MORE

Hyde, Natalie. **Soil Erosion and How to Prevent It**. New York: Crabtree, 2010.

Maloof, Torrey. **Weathering and Erosion**. Huntington Beach, Calif.: Teacher Created Materials, 2015.

Riley, Joelle. **Examining Erosion**. Minneapolis: Lerner Publications Co., 2013.

WEBSITES

Earth Science for Kids: Erosion
www.ducksters.com/science/earth_science/erosion.php
Read science facts about erosion and erosion control that people can do.

National Geographic Encyclopedia: Erosion
http://education.nationalgeographic.com/encyclopedia/erosion/
View a photo gallery, read about the different types of erosion, and watch a video about erosion on the coast of Alaska.

One Geology: Kids
www.onegeology.org/extra/kids/earthprocesses/deltas.html
See pictures and read about the different kinds of deltas that form because of water erosion.

Every effort has been made to ensure that these websites are appropriate for children. However, because of the nature of the Internet, it is impossible to guarantee that these sites will remain active indefinitely or that their contents will not be altered.

UPWORD INK PUBLISHING COMPANY©

"We write words to lift you up."

Connect with the World of Mrs. Ashbury in one of the ways below:

 WWW.MRSASHBURYSWORLD.COM 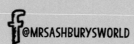 @MRSASHBURYSWORLD 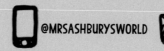 @MRSASHBURYSWORLD  MRSASHBURYTHEBOOKCHARACTER@GMAIL.COM

Mrs. Ashbury's Birthday

Written by: Rekia Beverly

Illustrated by: Donald L. Hill, MBA

Printed in the United States of America
ISBN-13: 978-1985622265

Dedication:

To Mom and Dad, thank you for everything.

"Boys and girls, I have an announcement to make. We have about 20 minutes left in the day, and I need you to clean up. Check your mailboxes, get your lunch boxes and backpack, then meet me on the carpet."

All the students quickly cleaned up in order for Mrs. Ashbury to make her announcement. Eagerly, the students sat on the carpet. "Tomorrow, I will be celebrating my birthday!" said Mrs. Ashbury. The class erupted with cheers.

Every student raised their hand, but Mrs. Ashbury only chose one student to call on.

"Yes, Rhonda?" said Mrs. Ashbury. In a soft voice, Rhonda said, "What would you like for your birthday? I got nail polish for my birthday and a lot of cupcakes, and all of my friends were invited to my birthday party."

Rhonda could hardly get her last word out before Ralphie interrupted, "Who cares about what you got for your birthday, Rhonda? I had a motor cross birthday party, and I had hundreds of people at my party." Rhonda's face drew sad.

Mrs. Ashbury was disappointed that Ralphie interrupted Rhonda while she was trying to share. In a kind and patient voice, Mrs. Ashbury explained to Ralphie that everyone could share their birthday story during writing time tomorrow and that he should be careful of his tone when speaking to his classmates.

"Sometimes you can say words to other people, but how you say it can truly hurt someone's feelings," said Mrs. Ashbury. She addressed the problem and redirected the conversation back to her celebration. After all, she wanted to include her students for her birthday.

"Okay, let's get back to my birthday celebration. I want to bring cupcakes for the class," Mrs. Ashbury said. All of the students started dancing. Mrs. Ashbury smiled and giggled. "You all are hilarious!" she said.

"Let's cast a vote! Who would like me to bring strawberry cupcakes? Raise your hand," Mrs. Ashbury said. She began to count, "1,2,3,4,5,6,7." "Next, who would like vanilla cupcakes?" - She counted the students who wanted vanilla 1,2,3 – "Lastly, who wants chocolate cupcakes? 1, 2," she asked.

"Mrs. Ashbury used her phone to type the students' responses.

The bell rang, and the students left for the day. Mrs. Ashbury packed her things. She went to the grocery store to buy the ingredients to bake cupcakes for her class.

She bought flour, confectioners' sugar, eggs, oil, and cupcake liners. (She remembered Rhonda was vegan, so she used a banana instead of eggs for her cupcake).

Mrs. Ashbury left the store and headed home.

When she got home, she put her apron on, washed her hands before cooking, and then started mixing the ingredients in her mixer. *Wow, these are going to be amazing,* she thought. *I'll add sprinkles to the vanilla cupcakes and put a Strawberry on top of the strawberry and chocolate cupcakes... maybe drizzle fudge on top.*

Mrs. Ashbury got the cupcake pan out of the cabinet, poured the batter into the pans and placed them in the oven and then set the timer for 1 hour and 45 minutes. Mrs. Ashbury started singing "Bake bake baking baking cupcakes, bake bake baking my students some cupcakes."

Mrs. Ashbury decided to sit in her favorite spot in her house - her recliner. Tick tock tick tock. The cupcakes were in the oven baking, and Mrs. Ashbury could feel herself getting tired, so she decided to grade papers. Tick tock tick tock. Time was passing by, and the timer hadn't gone off to let her know the cupcakes were done. Dingggggg!

Mrs. Ashbury paused from grading papers to go take out the delicious cupcakes she baked. Mrs. Ashbury cried "OH MY! The-the cupcakes are burnt!" *How will I be able to celebrate my birthday with my students now?* she thought.

The next day at school, she greeted her students at the door. Almost every student asked when it would be cupcake time. She told the students she would talk to them during morning meeting time.

All of the students joined her on the carpet. "Boys and girls," (in a sad voice) I set the timer too long for the cupcakes, and they burned," Mrs. Ashbury said. Rhonda raised her hand and said "It's ok, Mrs. Ashbury. We've all made a mistake before." Ralphie chimed in again, and this time, his tone was different. "Yeah, Mrs. Ashbury, it's ok. One time I baked cookies with my grandma, and she burned them, and my grandpa said no more baking for you," he said. Mrs. Ashbury smiled.

Ralphie had one more thing to say; "I saved half of my peanut butter and jelly sandwich for lunch. We can sing to you, and we can share my half with everyone." Mrs. Ashbury chuckled. "It's ok, Ralphie. You save your peanut butter and jelly. You all singing to me is all I need," she said. And so Rhonda and Ralphie lead the class in singing, "Happy birthday dear Mrs. Ashbury. Happy birthday to you."

Mrs. Ashbury realized her students loved her for who she is, not because she was making them cupcakes.

That was Mrs. Ashbury's best birthday ever!

Questions & Activities

1.) Who are the characters in the story?

_____

_____

2.) Write and draw about a time you had a problem and how was the problem solved.

_____

_____

_____

_____

Questions & Activities

3.) Write and draw how would you feel if someone interrupted you while you were talking?

_____

_____

Questions & Activities

4a.) If Mrs. Ashbury baked 7 strawberry cupcakes, 3 vanilla cupcakes, and 2 chocolate cupcakes. How many cupcakes did she bake in all? _____

4b.) If Mrs. Ashbury baked 7 strawberry cupcakes, 3 vanilla cupcakes, and 2 chocolate cupcakes, but 2 cupcakes burned.

How many cupcakes does Mrs. Ashbury have left? _____

ABOUT THE AUTHOR

Mrs. Ashbury is the brainchild of career educator and writer, Rekia Beverly.
A native of New Smyrna Beach, Florida.
Mrs. Ashbury is dear to Beverly's heart because many of her shared experiences with students are modeled after her actual teaching encounters.
Beverly created Mrs. Ashbury's character as a tool to empower students and parents with a different perspective of how teachers actually view themselves.
Her goal is to give awareness to readers that teachers live normal lives too. They are excited, unsure, and learn lessons throughout the year just like their students.
Beverly is pleased to share Mrs. Ashbury with families and students. Her dream is to continue the adventures of Mrs. Ashbury's class for many years to come.

To connect with Rekia Beverly or inquire about media please reach out to:
mrsashburythebookcharacter@gmail.com
upwordink@gmail.com.

24883271R00020

Made in the USA
Middletown, DE
21 December 2018